TABLE OF CONTENTS

IF I MET KIM KARDASHIAN

IF I MET KIM KARDASHIAN

1

Learning

A petite beauty with a stomach as flat as the back of a pan has cleared the path so others can follow. She has turned the old perception that queens who look like her have nothing upstairs on its head. For so long many had been made to believe those with a pretty face was all they had. Well, not this one, she has displayed unparalleled brilliance. She has made enough money to wage a war against a small country.

Her tools for success were the exact same things that attracted all the hate from those who frown when they hear her name. Everyone knows about her sweet voice that has a tendency to nourish hearts but capture the attentiveness of those who matter because it's worth listening to. Then that charming personality and persuasiveness that gets the deal done. You can't forget the powerful smile that has opened the minds of business executives and kept their attention.

Even the most principled in business will tell you about the importance of maintaining eye contact to keep the focus where it's needed. She has that too. What is there not to learn from this success story?

Not only is she the face of a brand, she is a mogul, a global brand; making her an example of a modern day mobile business. Wherever she is that's where her office is at. Work and life for her are intertwined. In graduate business school they teach learners to learn from people like her who have walked the path.

Success stories like her are in a better position to explain why they walked the path they walked. The elements in their lives at that time that made them walk that particular path. How they were sure, if they were, that the timing was right to walk the path they did. The challenges they faced along the way. What they did to rid themselves of the challenges and what they think they should have done better had they known what they know now.

People in her position can usually see what the rest of us cannot. They can bring awareness to us the opportunities they believe are being ignored which they think those who want to write the same story as they did should focus on and exploit.

There's no doubt about it, she is a walking graduate business class that should be taken seriously by those who want to achieve even a portion of the success she has achieved. To become who she is there is reason to be sure she has gone through the mill and is now a fountain of wisdom because of it. This wisdom is what people like me would want to make an effort to learn from.

While not polite it's fair if someone were to conclude that such a sense of reasoning is sad. There are a million ways to win in life. Everyone has their own way. I believe learning from those who have already walked the path and succeeded makes life a little bit easier; regardless of what some may say.

I will be honest I've had days where I couldn't see where I was going. My future was dark, it looked totally blank. I felt spent and had no idea what to do next. I was completely clueless. There was a gulf between where I was and where I needed to be. The distance was vast and I didn't know how to close the gap. It would be beautiful to know if she ever felt as clueless as I have sometimes felt about myself. It would be encouraging to know if she has ever felt inept before in her life. How she kept pushing and what motivated her that indeed there was light at the end of the tunnel.

I'm certain I'm not alone in this; I can't be the only one who is curious to know if she has ever been in these situations before. I believe there are a lot of us who have been to a point where we knew we had given 100% of our efforts to an initiative only to get backslapped by life at every turn. Life can be cruel like that. Has life been cruel like that to her too?

Personally, I started a business that tanked. I gave it 100% of what I had in terms of focus, time, energy and money. Unfortunately, nothing came of it. Everything that could have gone wrong with it went wrong. The timing, the economic downturn, Covid 19, I mean you can name it; it was there on the unending list. I got overwhelmed fighting fires all the time and couldn't save the business. All my efforts were just not sufficient. Putting out fires eventually got exhausting. I couldn't win. So, I decided to shut it down. It was the most humiliating and humbling feeling ever.

In business school they teach that for every successful person that you see 9 times out of 10 they have failed numerous times and found a way to keep going. Did she fail numerous times too? I would really want to know if she has failed before and whether it was as defeating as it felt for me. I have suffered some heavy defeats and moving on from them was a huge task. There were times I would think I had recovered only to suffer some more monumental defeats again. I was fortunate enough to have not lost my mind because I was so close.

The new thing in business nowadays is networking. Before she became a business like she is now did she have a wide business network? I would want to know this because especially when you are starting, it seems like you're all alone. How to get from ground zero where you don't know any relevant person that can help to a point where you have a wide network can sometimes be scientific. I know she's sociable and all but I think building a business network is different. How did she get that business network?

Of course, she's more social than I am. Our personality contexts are different. What I'm trying to say here is; people don't even like me. I would want to know what she would suggest for those people who can hardly make any friends like me. How does she suggest we go about it? Social media is not even our thing. There are a lot of us out there. What do we need to do to have a wider network that is relevant? I must add, business school doesn't teach that part. You pretty-much have to figure it out on your own.

People always say you should network but getting to know those who matter is not as easy as it sounds. There's a path you need to follow a path less successful people like myself have not grasped as yet. I have heard a marketing guru say you should fake it till you make it. What a dish of potatoes. Does that really work? Some of these catchy phrases sound so good when you're exchanging them at a birthday party, but in a business setting they can be suicidal.

The way I see it; a lot of people have been lied to all their lives and are just sick of people who con their way into their hearts and minds. Nobody likes being taken for a fool. I have interacted with a fair share of people who do not like people who claim to be who they're not. I would ask Kim what she thinks about this and if people can see through the lies when you're trying to fake it till you make it and whether it would not put them off.

Personally, I just don't trust fake people. If what I see before me is a false presentation how am I to know the real person? Maybe that's why I'm not as successful as she is. Maybe I should learn to fake it till I make it too.

She has to have encountered numerous characters that did the same. By now she has formed an opinion about such people. Instead of me putting a lot of time reinventing the wheel I would rather learn from her because I believe her thoughts count. If she has not done it before I'm certain in her numerous interactions with business clients or partners she has run into people who did it to her. I'm curious to know whether she saw through it all and how it made her feel. Understanding her thoughts would give critical insights into how other relevant people would likely feel as well.

There are a lot of things to learn from her. It would be of value to learn how she handled situations when she was caught unprepared or when she didn't know what she was expected to know at particular moments in her life. She is a human being like the rest of us. I'm sure there were times when she was not equipped with what most people would call the right responses. What did she do?

There are ways to cleverly handle yourself in such situations where you don't have sufficient information to respond to certain questions. Clever people always offer smart responses even in dire circumstances. They do so because they have mastered the art. I want to learn how to master the art too. Everybody wants to appear smart.

Depending on the business setting, incorrect or insufficient responses at inappropriate times can be costly. There's no better way to learn how to avoid this than to learn from the experiences of others who have been there and done it. By virtue of being a businessperson she has been part of many presentations made to her as a global brand or part of the executive team of her company. She has seen many get caught up in such moments and should have tips that are game changing.

Activism

I have been fortunate to have visited a few countries but I was born in Zimbabwe. It's possible she probably has never head of Zimbabwe in her life but I'm about to let her know why I would want her to know more about this lovely country if I met her. Before I do that I have to remind everyone that she is an activist who fights for those unfairly disadvantaged. I'm not making this up, it's all documented. Not only that she's also a lawyer. This is relevant to understand where I'm about to take this.

Zimbabwe is a small country of about 15 million citizens and is located in the southern part of Africa. It was put on sanctions in the year 2001 by the United States of America at the instigation of Britain. This was achieved through an act that was enacted through congress culminating in what is known as the ZIDERA law.

This law prohibits American businesses from doing business with any of the Zimbabwean companies, the Zimbabwean government and certain individuals. It basically restricts any type of business between citizens, the governments and companies of the two countries. Defying the sanctions is punishable by law not limited to bank accounts being frozen by OFAC (Office of Foreign Assets and Control). Attorneys would be in a better position to break down the ZIDERA law in detail but in summary that's what it does.

This law has been effective for the better part of more than the last two decades. To put the ZIDERA law into effect there was collusion between United States of America and a majority of Western nations. They made a pact that none of the countries involved would do business with the Zimbabwe government, its people or its companies. If they did then the United States of America would not do business with them as well.

Children who were born and grew up in this period have to this day finished college and some have started their own families. All they know is life under sanctions. They don't know any better. The reason I bring Zimbabwe up is I have seen Kim work with the United States of America government to help free people who had spent almost all of their entire adult lives incarcerated for crimes they did not commit. She gave them hope and delivered on that hope. There are a number of Americans who benefitted from her efforts who now have a reason to live again because of what she did for them.

She took the challenge to free wrongly incarcerated Americans and conquered. Now, why not take the fight for freeing a people internationally? She has already proven she can handle her own with stiff challenges. While challenges across the world can never be all surmounted, a whole nation needs her. Apart from making a lot of money I believe this would be the greatest satisfying win for her amongst all she has succeeded in doing. Rescuing a nation from the jaws of poverty! Nothing can beat that.

Zimbabwe needs the same fight from Kim. For so long, Zimbabwe has been striving to have a person who could ignite that conversation for the plight of the people to be heard. A person like Kim who is eager to see the world treat the little guy fairly and if not, will get a fight of their lives. The citizens of Zimbabwe have suffered for too long and are looking for a new way forward. Zimbabweans dream of the day when Kim selects Zimbabwe as who she will fight for next to remove sanctions that have outlived their use.

The economy has been screaming for more than two decades. Those who could weep did so until they could do it no more. Life has been that painful. Graveyards are filled with people who were stressed till they chose to go under. Many of those are six feet in the ground. They could no longer feed not only their families, but they could not feed themselves either.

The question then becomes, when are those who championed for sanctions to be enforced going to feel the lessons they were trying to teach the country have been taught? It seems like their thirst to see poverty, destitution, hunger and restlessness in a people will never be quenched.

Zimbabwe has no option than to turn to Kim. The country has indeed learned a lesson or two albeit the tough way. Even in this current moment, because the sanctions still prevail, Zimbabwe is currently still living the lessons of those teachings. Zimbabwe deserves to have Kim as its advocate for a better future. Sanctions must now go, unconditionally.

Honestly, who benefits when poor people who are already eking a living suffer even more? The United Nations itself has in no uncertain terms said these sanctions are illegal because they did not go through the supreme body of the United Nations.

The question probably would be what do I want Kim to do about it? Well, there's an easy answer to that although it will be lengthy for clarity. If given the opportunity Zimbabwe has enough natural resources to pivot itself into a prosperous country. The reason why Zimbabwe has not achieved prosperity has been because it's sitting on natural resources and cannot get them exploited to benefit the nation and her citizens.

Companies that have the technology and financial muscle among other factors needed to exploit these natural resources majority of them are in the West. They can't come to Zimbabwe to exploit these natural resources to improve the economies of both Zimbabwe and the outside world because of the sanctions. The natural resources are there but investment is needed from companies that have the technology, knowhow and financial wherewithal to extract the minerals, process and value add them. This is what will create industries and get the citizens employed.

To illustrate further, let me give one example of the minerals in abundance in the country. Zimbabwe is in the top 5 in the world in terms of countries with high lithium deposits. Lithium is a mineral used to make lithium batteries. The future of cars is in electric vehicles. Electric vehicles use lithium batteries. It would be expensive for the final consumer if car battery companies were to buy lithium used in making the lithium batteries from third parties. Car battery companies need to have plants in countries like Zimbabwe where the natural resource is so they can manufacture their own car batteries.

Zimbabwe is ready to do business with car battery companies or any other car company supply chains from anywhere in the world who want to invest in mining or in the value addition of the mineral. What this would do is the car battery companies would be able to produce their own batteries which they would sell to car companies at a price that makes sense to them. Zimbabwe would benefit in that its citizens would get employed and the government would get added revenue through taxes. An employed populace spends money resulting in economic growth. This is not happening because of the sanctions.

Remember, lithium is not only restricted to making car batteries. All kinds of batteries are made from lithium that is from cell phone batteries to solar light batteries. Car batteries were just used as an example. Lithium has other uses as well apart from the manufacture of batteries.

Kim would be the next thing to a Messiah if she managed to get the sanctions removed from Zimbabwe. This is just one mineral that I have discussed. Zimbabwe has majority of the minerals found beneath the earth's surface. These are not limited to gold, diamonds and platinum. There are plenty more.

Simply put, as an activist who champions fighting for the people. Zimbabwe would be grateful if she fought for her citizens too. If there's a person that can get sanctions removed from Zimbabwe it's her. She has gone to battle for a lot of individual Americans. I'm sure she would find a challenge in breaking a record or two stepping it up to the next level, putting an entire nation on her back.

Zimbabwe has been under the yoke of sanctions for the better part of more than two decades. If there's a country and its people that deserve her efforts, it's this African country Zimbabwe and its people. The Zimbabwean population has suffered enough.

Yes, Zimbabwe erred when it tried to correct artificial imbalances made by the British settlers who pushed indigenous Zimbabweans to infertile soils but the error has since been corrected.

Just to give her a brief background on how Zimbabwe was put on sanctions. Zimbabwe was a British colony. At that time before independence it was known as Rhodesia. It became a colony because of how it was endowed with natural resources which included but were not limited to minerals and a vast amount of land. When the country became a colony, prime land was forcibly taken by the British settlers from the indigenous people. This meant that the majority indigenous people were pushed into infertile soils that were not suitable for agriculture.

Zimbabwe being an agrarian economy, an economy where its citizens primarily survive on agriculture; what the British settlers did created a cycle of poverty in the indigenous citizens because they were now failing to feed themselves among many things. Inevitably, this led to a war of liberation against the settlers with indigenous people fighting primarily to reclaim their land. The indigenous people won the liberation war that made them independent in 1980 and changed the name of the country to Zimbabwe.

However, the British reneged on the agreement that was brokered prior to the ceasefire. That agreement is known as the Lancaster House Peace Agreement. The agreement stated that Britain would compensate farmers who were the descendants of the British settlers for the land and the improvements that had been done on the land that the indigenous people had been disenfranchised on. When the British Government was approached at a later date to abide by the Lancaster House Peace Agreement, the government of the day which was from a different political affiliation from the one that participated in the agreement disowned the Lancaster House Peace Agreement. They refused to obey what was in the agreement.

After numerous failed discussions Zimbabwe was left with no option as its citizens pushed the government between 1999 and 2000 to have land reform. Land reform was primarily the process of taking back the land from the descendents of the British settlers who had not purchased the land but inherited stolen land and giving it back to its rightful owners.

However, to the world it was told as if white people were under attack. The narrative that was pushed by the media was white people were having their farms taken by the black African government without any compensation. Land that was taken from about 4,000 of the white farmers was distributed to about 350,000 households. These farms were huge, they were large tracts of land, and majority of them were well over 2,000ha a piece.

These 350, 000 households were given this land divided into A1 or A2 farms and communal farmers. A1 and A2 farms were allocations of farms depending on the size of the farms. The sizes were determined by many things from farming experience to education in agriculture or its value chains. Communal farmers were mainly given land to farm to feed themselves and their families then maybe sell the surplus.

Coincidentally, the United States of America needed the support of Britain in the war against Iraq. Britain through its Prime Minister then Tony Blair said it would support United States of America only if United States of America supported Britain in bringing untold sanctions to Zimbabwe. This was under the claim that Zimbabwe was taking land from white farmers without any compensation. That's how President George Bush was convinced to collude with other Western nations to apply sanctions on Zimbabwe as a country and its leaders. Prior to Prime Minister Tony Blair approaching George Bush, Zimbabwe and United States of America never had any differences.

The sanctions placed on Zimbabwe by President George Bush and his allies were primarily at the instigation of the then Prime Minister of Britain, Tony Blair. However,

Zimbabwe has since acknowledged that the farmers should have been compensated for the improvements made on the farms. Yes, Britain reneged on the Lancaster House Peace Agreement to compensate the farmers but the farmers needed to be compensated for the improvements made on the farms regardless.

Modalities have now been put in place to compensate the farmers for the improvements they made on the farms. An agreement between the government and the farmers has already been struck for the farmers to be compensated to a sum total of USD$3.5 billion. This initiative will put to rest the land distribution issue.

There's absolutely no doubt she can pull this off. If she managed to free people who had been incarcerated for many decades; people who were still looking at serving many more years to come behind bars, especially for crimes they did not commit. This is a challenge she can tackle. It might be a little bit different but she has been there before and I have absolute confidence in her abilities.

Victoria Falls

Well, I would also tell her Zimbabwe is not just about grim stories. In fact the leadership has been championing engagement and re-engagement. Zimbabwe is a friend to all and an enemy to none. Being the businesswoman she is her typical days are filled with fighting fires from all angles.

She needs relaxing time. Zimbabwe has that too. Zimbabwe is home to the seventh wonder of the world. The majestic Victoria falls. It is a must-have on the bucket list. If the right time is picked she can run into the festival which is done on a yearly basis. It's normally done over a few days. It attracts many regulars from across the world including a lot from the United States of America.

I'm not sure if she is an adrenaline junkie but if she is Victoria Falls is the right spot for her. She can take advantage of the gorges there to go for bungee jumping among the activities to partake in. She can also tour the area in a helicopter and have a bird's eye view at how magnificent the whole place looks from above. This has been a highlight for many tourists I'm certain it would be for her too.

There's also an activity called water rafting if she's familiar with it. She can do this with guides who will help her get around pressure points in the water as they go from one point to the other.

4

The Big 5

There are animals that are found in Zimbabwe that she has probably never seen live ever before. Zimbabwe is home to the Big 5. These are the lion, the rhinoceros, the African buffalo, the leopard and the elephant. Even if she's not a wildlife person just watching how huge and athletic some of these beasts are is an otherworldly feeling that I'm certain she would get a thrill out of. While there are numerous places in Zimbabwe where the Big 5 can be found, for the best experience I would recommend Hwange National Park. It's close to Victoria Falls as well.

5

Nyanga

From there she can fly to Nyanga, a mountainous area known among other things for its zip line activities where she can zip from one mountain to another. It's not for the faint of hearts though. Everyone who knows anything about her knows she also loves the water. This is the place where she can have primetime moments because it's good for those who have fallen in love with the camera. Miniature falls in this area are in large numbers she can pick the best where she can have photo-shoots under streaming falls.

6

Influencer

Put together Kim and her family have a following almost the size of the whole of Africa. I'm not a dummy. As a writer, if I met her I would be a complete fool if I didn't at least ask her to promote my content. Not all of it, just one of her choice. The family she comes from is a closely knit family I would have to ask her if she could let some of her family members ask their fans to buy or at the minimum critic my content. This includes her fans as well.

Of the short stories I've written I would give her a choice of seven good ones to pick from to promote at least one, **CRAWLING FROM A DEEP HOLE** by Martin Majaji, **KNOW YOUR VALUE** by Martin Majaji, **YOU CAN'T FORGET PAIN** by Martin Majaji, **TAKING GATHERING NEW KNOWLEDGE TOO FAR** by Martin Majaji, **HARD CHOICES** by Martin Majaji, **HARD DECISIONS** by Martin Majaji and **PUMPKIN** by Martin Majaji all available on www.amazon.com

7

Alternative markets

Back to business Kim owns a few companies including SKIMS which is into swimwear. Zimbabwe grows some of the best cotton in the world. What this means is the cotton to make the best fabric and ultimately the best clothes is available. Zimbabwe is exporting majority of this cotton in its raw form to other countries who end up value adding to the cotton to make fabric and clothes. Then Zimbabwe imports the fabric and clothes at an expensive price. This is where I believe Kim could get involved.

Zimbabwe is filled with talented people. The country is just teeming with graduates who are waiting for opportunities. She can team-up with local textile companies for expansion or build a factory in Zimbabwe that takes advantage of the raw material available locally and make fabric that suits her needs which will later be used to make her swimwear. It could be for the SKIMS brand or any other brand that she can wish to come up with. Costs for production are cheap in Zimbabwe. Factories built in economic zones enjoy various forms of incentives that she can take advantage of.

Zimbabwe is the perfect place to make her swimwear or any other products made from fabric. Besides, Zimbabwe is a peaceful country where there is no disruption to business.

Zimbabwe would be a perfect place to establish offices for her businesses on the continent. From Zimbabwe it would be easier to access other markets within the continent from North, East, West to South.

In the southern part of Africa where Zimbabwe is located there's a community of nations known as the Southern African Development Community (SADC) which consists of 15 countries and with a population market of almost 380 million people. Zimbabwe is centrally located making it sufficient to be a distribution hub. From SADC it would be easier to penetrate the rest of the African market which has a combined market of close to 1, 2 billion people. Swimwear has only been mentioned because it's the popular one among her business empire but the same can be applied to whatever pleases her to invest in Zimbabwe.

8

Personal note

If I met Kim I would talk to her about all of these things. It's out of appreciation of her as a person. My acknowledgement of how much of a fighter she is when her activist blood is flowing through her body is on another level. She has my full respect and would do wonders for the small nation in Africa called Zimbabwe. Unchaining Zimbabwe from sanctions would easily make her Zimbabwe's other mother. It would be a befitting title because she would have freed a nation from a future filled with struggle just like a mother would.

Not only that she is a humble businessperson and she's very human too. She has a wonderful support system and is always looking for new challenges. If I met her, this is the kind of discussion I would have with her. What would you do if you met a successful person whose work you admire, what would you say to them that would be decent enough not to annoy them or make them upset?

www.ingramcontent.com/pod-product-compliance
Lightning Source LLC
Chambersburg PA
CBHW051929250726
48659CB00002B/913